M000032602

For My Father

For My Father

Edited by Susan Feuer

Illustrated by Cindy Lindgren

Ariel Books

■ ■ ■

Andrews and McMeel
Kansas City

ISBN: 0-8362-1528-1

CONTENTS

INTRODUCTION

Wise musings, tidbits of advice, and fond recollections are gathered in this volume, which celebrates fathers and all they bring to our lives. The love that dads have for their children may be immeasurable—but it is easy to see. Carefully untangling our kite strings, proudly cheering us on at softball games, and patiently teaching us how to drive a manual transmission are all examples of fatherly devotion.

We admire our fathers so much as children and watch

everything they do with an unblinking gaze. We learn from them the importance of getting along with others and the value of saying "please" and "thank you." When we grow older, we constantly solicit their opinions and advice on a myriad of issues.

Unsung heroes, our fathers are at first our guides, then our friends as we journey through life. And no matter how long the journey, our fathers and our memories of them, enrich us every day.

FATHERLY ADVICE

We often seek our fathers' advice, but just as often they seem to sense when we are in need of a wise word or two. We can learn from our fathers just by watching them as they resolve conflicts within the family or deal with the challenges of everyday life. It is easy to assess the value of our fathers' advice because we know that our character would be weaker and our life less rich without the benefit of their teaching.

A good name and good advice is all your dad can give you.

—*Harry S. Truman*

You cannot teach a man anything; you can only help him find it within himself.

—*Galileo*

The quality of a person's life is in direct proportion to their commitment to excellence, regardless of their chosen field of endeavor.

—*Vince Lombardi*

Every one expects to go further than his father went; every one expects to be better than he was born and every generation has one big impulse in its heart—to exceed all the other generations of the past in all the things that make life worth living.

—*William Allen White*

You cannot run away from a weakness; you must sometime fight it out or perish. And if that be so, why not now, and where you stand?

—*Robert Louis Stevenson*

Don't limit a child to your own learning, for he was born in another time.

—*Rabbinical saying*

The tongue of experience has the most truth.

—*Arabic proverb*

Dad gave me two pieces of advice. One was, "No matter how good you think you are, there are people better than you." But he was an optimist too; his other advice: "Never worry about rejection. Every day is a new beginning."

—*John Ritter*

All that we [old poets] can do is to keep our heart as fresh as we may; to bear ever in mind that a father can guide a son but some distance on the road, and the more wisely he guides the sooner (alas!) must he lose the fair companionship and watch the boy run on. It may sound a hard saying, but we can only keep him admiring the things we admire at the cost of pauperizing his mind.

—*Sir Arthur Quiller-Couch*

Experience is not what happens to you; it is what you do with what happens to you.

—*Aldous Huxley*

You will find as you look back upon your life that the moments when you have really lived are the moments when you have done things in the spirit of love.

—*Henry Drummond*

Setting a good example for your children takes all the fun out of middle age.

—*William Feather*

Whatever you would have your children become, strive to exhibit in your own lives and conversation.

—*Lydia H. Sigourney*

A house full of people is a house full of different points of view.

—*Maori proverb*

Always go with people who are smarter than you are— and in your case it won't be difficult.

—*Francis Cardinal Spellman's father*

Enjoy when you can, and endure when you must.
— *Wolfgang von Goethe*

Don't demand respect, as a parent. Demand civility and insist on honesty. But respect is something you must earn— with kids as well as with adults.
— *William Attwood*

Your children need your presence more than your presents.
— *Jesse Jackson*

Never raise your hand to your children; it leaves your midsection unprotected.
— *Robert Orben*

The most important thing that parents can teach their children is how to get along without them.
— *Frank Clark*

The father who does not teach his son his duties is equally guilty with the son who neglects them.

—*Confucius*

Train a child in the way he should go, and when he is old he will not depart from it.

—*Proverbs 12:4*

Seek advice but use your own common sense.

—*Yiddish proverb*

In my younger and more vulnerable years my father gave me some advice I've been turning over in my mind ever since.

—*F. Scott Fitzgerald*

Never get sick, Hubert, there isn't time.

—*Hubert H. Humphrey's father*

It is better to bind your children to you by a feeling of respect, and by gentleness, than by fear.

—*Terence*

It is a wise father that knows his own child.

—*William Shakespeare*

What would life be if we had no courage to attempt anything?

—*Vincent van Gogh*

In order to live a good and clean life my father has taught me six basic rules:

If I don't do it, then you don't do it.

No one knows the truth but your conscience and God.

You are never a failure as long as you give it your best.

Do not forget your culture.

Do not do something just because I am around.

Education and honesty are two of the most important
    things you should have.

—*Dagem Hailemariam*

We make a living by what we get, but we make a life by what we give.

—*Norman MacEwan*

FAMILY LIFE

Gone is the stereotype of the father as the family's sole breadwinner and disciplinarian. Roles have blurred: now it might be dad who stays home with the newborn baby. It doesn't much matter which roles fathers play; what does matter is that they love us, comfort us, and make us feel secure. The love and respect we offer in return form a protective bond that encircles the family.

Romance fails us and so do friendships, but the relationship of parent and child, less noisy than all others, remains indelible and indestructible, the strongest relationship on earth.

—*Theodor Reik*

The best brought-up children are those who have seen their parents as they are. Hypocrisy is not the parents' first duty.

—*George Bernard Shaw*

What children say, they have heard at home.

—*Wolof (West African) proverb*

There is something ultimate in a father's love, something that cannot fail, something to be believed against the whole world.

—*Frederick W. Faber*

To maintain a joyful family requires much from both the parents and the children. Each member of the family has to become, in a special way, the servant of the others.

—*Pope John Paul II*

You don't have to deserve your mother's love. You have to deserve your father's. He's more particular.

—*Robert Frost*

There are only two lasting bequests we can hope to give our children. One of these is roots; the other, wings.

—*Hodding Carter*

The family—that dear octopus from whose tentacles we never quite escape, nor, in our inmost hearts, ever quite wish to.

—*Dodie Smith*

What children expect from grown-ups is not to be "understood," but only to be loved, even though this love may be expressed clumsily or in sternness. Intimacy does not exist between generations—only trust.

—*Carl Zucker*

Life is but one continual course of instruction. The hand of the parent writes on the heart of the child the first faint characters which time deepens into strength so that nothing can efface them.

—*R. Hill*

Reinforce the stitch that ties us, and I will do the same for you.

—*Doris Schwerin*

Family jokes, though rightly cursed by strangers, are the bond that keeps most families alive.

—*Stella Benson*

Anything which parents have not learned from experience they can now learn from their children.

—*Anonymous*

I had the total attention of both my parents, and was secure in the knowledge of being loved. . . . My memories of falling asleep at night are to the comfortable sound of my parents' voices, voices which conveyed in their tones the message that these two people loved and trusted one another.

—*Jill Ker Conway*

I happen to feel that total separation between parents and [adult] children is one of the great tragedies of our culture. Both generations really need the sustenance the other has to give and both are impoverished when the relationship does not continue.

—*Adelaide Bry*

Every parent is at some time the father of the unreturned prodigal, with nothing to do but keep his house open to hope.

—*John Ciardi*

When you have children, you begin to understand what you owe your parents.

—*Japanese proverb*

What families have in common the world around is that they are the place where people learn who they are and how to be that way.

—*Jean Illsley Clarke*

What we forget as children is that our parents are children, also. The child in them has not been satisfied or met or loved, often. Not always, but very often. Oftener, actually, than is admitted.

—*Edna O'Brien*

A baby has a way of making a man out of his father and a boy out of his grandfather.

—*Angie Papadakis*

As a substitute father for hundreds of youths over the past thirteen years, I have yet to encounter a young person in trouble whose difficulty could not be traced to the lack of a strong father image in the home.

—*Paul Anderson*

The most important thing a father can do for his children is to love their mother.

—*Theodore M. Hesburgh*

Allow children to be happy in their own way, for what better way will they ever find?

—*Samuel Johnson*

Fathers are what give daughters away to other men who aren't nearly good enough, so they can have grandchildren who are smarter than anybody's.

—*Paul Harvey*

It has always been economically and politically important for men to know that they are the fathers of their children.

—*Louise Bernikow*

To show a child what has once delighted you, to find the child's delight added to your own, so that there is now a double delight seen in the glow of trust and affection, this is happiness.

—*J. B. Priestley*

The family is the nucleus of civilization.

—*Will and Ariel Durant*

How easily a father's tenderness is recalled, and how quickly a son's offenses vanish at the slightest word of repentance!

—*Molière*

The thing that impresses me most about America is the way parents obey their children.

— *Duke of Windsor*

Fathers see babies as potentially grown-up—they are more likely than mothers to transform their perception of their newborn into fantasies about the adult it will become, and about the things they (father and child) will be able to do together when the infant is much older.

— *Dorothy Burlingham*

Fathers are blind to the faults of their daughters.

— *Saying*

Children have never been very good at listening to their elders, but they have never failed to imitate them.

— *James Baldwin*

An atmosphere of trust, love, and humor can nourish extraordinary human capacity. One key is authenticity: parents acting as people, not as roles.

— *Marilyn Ferguson*

The great danger for family life, in the midst of any society whose idols are pleasure, comfort, and independence, lies in the fact that people close their hearts and become selfish.

—*Pope John Paul II*

Fatherhood ought to be emphasized as much as motherhood. The idea that women are solely responsible for deciding whether or not to have babies leads on to the idea that they are also responsible for bringing the children up.

—*Shirley Williams*

To become a father is not hard,
To be a father is, however.

—*Wilhelm Busch*

MEMORIES OF DAD

aybe it's his huge hands or his booming laugh that stick in our memory, maybe it's the time he taught us to play checkers. Of all the thousands of memories we have of our fathers, we usually cherish a handful above all others. When we are children, our fathers loom larger than life—they are giants who can repair any toy and solve any problem. When we are adults, our fathers shrink back down to life-size and our perceptions of them are different. Regardless of our age, however, we cherish the memories of our dads as much as we cherish them.

I talk and talk and talk, and I haven't taught people in fifty years what my father taught by example in one week.

—*Mario Cuomo*

On my twenty-first birthday my father said, "Son, here's a million dollars. Don't lose it."

—*Larry Niven*

Dad often said, "A man that doesn't pick up a penny that's laying on the ground won't ever amount to much." And if I'm not mistaken, the statement was prefaced by, "I remember my dad always saying . . ." So I'm the third (at least) generation to have received this wisdom.

—*Ric Anderson*

Dad taught me never to settle for anything less than what I want. I think that's what made him so great. He always promotes that image of being such a tyrant, but the truth is, there couldn't be a sweeter father.

—*Victoria Preminger*

My father taught me to read from one of those first-grade readers. "Oh my," said Dick. "See Spot run." My father reacted right away, taking a bright red pencil, crossing out the "Oh my's" and writing in "Odds bodkins," "Gadzooks," "Gorblimey," and such all down the page. It was a revelation. It was the opposite of boring. The possibilities seemed endless and wonderful and I think it was at that moment I became a writer.

—*Gordon Chaplin*

Every day of my life has been a gift from him. His lap had been my refuge from lightning and thunder. His arms had sheltered me from teenage heartbreak. His wisdom and understanding had sustained me as an adult.

—*Nellie Pike Randall*

My father was as compulsive and efficient as I am. At Saturday morning breakfast, he would give each of us a list of chores that we had to get done for the day before any free time. My mother would get very upset when she got a list.

—*David Fissel*

I learned from the example of my father that the manner in which one endures what must be endured is more important than the thing that must be endured.

—*Dean Acheson*

My dad was always there for me and my brother, and I want my kids to have the same kind of dad—a dad they will remember. Being a dad is the most important thing in my life.

—*Kevin Costner*

It's only when you grow up, and step back from him, or leave him for your own career and your own home—it's only then that you can measure his greatness and fully appreciate it. Pride reinforces love.

—*Margaret Truman, on her father, Harry S. Truman*

How would I describe my father? Cool. He's cool. He's learned. He knows a lot of stuff.

—*Wynton Marsalis*

My earliest recollections are of being dressed up and allowed to come down to dance for a group of gentlemen who applauded and laughed as I pirouetted before them. Finally, my father would pick me up and hold me high in the air. He dominated my life as long as he lived, and was the love of my life for many years after he died.

—*Eleanor Roosevelt*

Papa was a man of brimstone and hot fire, in his mind and in his fists, and was known . . . as the champion of all the fist fighters. He used his fists on sharks and fakers, and all to give his family nice things.
—*Woody Guthrie*

There have been many times when I thought other people might be better singers or better musicians or prettier than me, but then I would hear Daddy's voice telling me to never say never, and I would find a way to squeeze an extra inch or two out of what God had given me.
—*Barbara Mandrell*

We were very poor, so my father worked two jobs at a time, sometimes three. So he wasn't home that much. On Christmas morning we would have to wait upstairs while he finished his milk deliveries before going down to open our presents. But he was a sweet man, very loving. He took the time to do things with his kids. I think he taught by example, rather than by direct advice.
—*Sam Wynkoop*

My father was two men, one sympathetic and intuitional, the other critical and logical; altogether they formed a combination that could not be thrown off its feet.

—*Julian Hawthorne, on his father, Nathaniel Hawthorne*

When I was a boy of fourteen, my father was so ignorant I could hardly stand to have the old man around. But when I got to be twenty-one, I was astonished at how much he had learned in seven years.

—*Mark Twain*

My best training came from my father.

—*Woodrow Wilson*

I remember being at a point below his knees and looking up at the vast length of him. He was six foot three; his voice was big. He was devastatingly attractive—even to his daughter as a child. . . . His voice was so beautiful, so enveloping. He was just bigger and better than anyone else.

—*Anjelica Huston, on her father, John Huston*

He [my father] also emphasized that a man's dignity lives after him; it's what you contribute to this world that matters, not what you take out of it. The essence of love is not to be loved but to give love.

—*Ricardo Montalban*

I wanted him to cherish and approve of me, not as he had when I was a child, but as the woman I was, who had her own mind and had made her own choices.

—*Adrienne Rich*

As a Man Grows Older
He values the voice of experience more and the voice of
  prophecy less.
He finds more of life's wealth in the common pleasures—
  home, health, children.
He thinks more about worth of men and less about their
  wealth.
He begins to appreciate his own father a little more.
He boasts less and boosts more.
He hurries less, and usually makes more progress.
He esteems the friendship of God a little higher.

—*Roy L. Smith*

Oh, the comfort, the inexpressible comfort of feeling safe with a person, having neither to weigh thoughts nor measure words, but pouring them all right out, just as they are, chaff and grain together; certain that a faithful hand will take and sift them, keep what is worth keeping, and then with the breath of kindness throw the rest away.
—*Dinah Maria Mulock Craik*

My dad is the backbone of our family. Any problem that I've ever had, he's always been there for me.
—*Whitney Houston*

I remember being upset once and telling my dad I wasn't following through right, and he replied, "Nancy, it doesn't make any difference to a ball what you do after you hit it."
—*Nancy Lopez*

My father was the dominant person in our family and in my life.
—*Jimmy Carter*

My prescription for success is based on something my father always used to tell me: you should never try to be better than someone else, but you should never cease trying to be the best that you can be.

—*John Wooden*

I remember my father's final lesson. My boy will learn by what I am and what I do far more than by what I tell him.

—*Norman Lewis Smith*

My father taught me to be honest, to do the best job I could do, and to be fair to whomever I was dealing with. Whenever I worked for anyone, he always insisted I see the job through. He would not let me quit until the job was finished. He taught me good manners and how to be a gentleman. After twenty-five years of marriage, I still hold the door for my wife.

—*Harry Steele*

Fathers are something else. They always give up their turn by saying something like, "Go ask your mother. She knows about things like that."

—*Mary Kuczkir*

I just owe almost everything to my father [and] it's passionately interesting for me that the things that I learned in a small town, in a very modest home, are just the things that I believe have won the election.

—*Margaret Thatcher*

Our father, while he lived, had cast a magic over everything, for us as well as for her. He held his love up over us like an umbrella and kept off the troubles that afterward came down on us, pouring cats and dogs!

—*Mary Lavin*

My father was very strong. I don't agree with a lot of the ways he brought me up. I don't agree with a lot of his values, but he did have a lot of integrity, and if he told us not to do something, he didn't do it either.

—*Madonna*

There is magic in the moment, for when I open my eyes and see my sons in the place where my father once sat, I feel an invisible bond between our three generations, an anchor of loyalty linking my sons to the grandfather whose face they never saw but whose person they have already come to know through this most timeless of all sports, baseball.

—*Doris Kearns Goodwin*

He had the precious gift of being deaf when convenient. Many people took this for absent-mindedness, but it was rather his faculty for concentrating on what suited him . . . in order to grasp reality better he limited his perceptions to a few definite things.

—*Jean Renoir*

My father, who was in politics, told me to remain a bit mysterious. A good friend and father figure to him gave him this advice. It makes people wonder about you, draws them to you as we are all drawn to a mystery.

—*Joe Mills*

Father was never late. Indeed, punctuality was his eleventh commandment. He saw lateness as a signal to the boss that you didn't care about your job, a potentially suicidal misstep. "If you're to be there at seven," he lectured me, "you be there at six forty-five. And you don't go to the water bucket more than once an hour."

—*Dan Rather*

One night at about two o'clock in the morning my father caught a man stealing bananas from our backyard. He went over to the man with his machete, took the bananas, cut the bunch in half and said, "Here, you can have it." And then he said, "From now on, if you need anything from the back of our house, come to the front."

—*Chi Chi Rodriguez*

When I was a child, my father taught me to put up my fists like a boy and to be prepared to defend myself at all times.

—*Camille Paglia*

What a father says to his children is not heard by the world, but it will be heard by posterity.

—*Jean Paul Richter*

This book was set in Dolman.

Heliotype. and Bembo.

———————

Designed and typeset by Junie Lee